D1560556

This book is for UX UI Designers and Developers to
sketch wireframes and make notes about their projects.

Copyright © 2022 by Martina Steg.

First paperback edition January 2022

www.purple-lemon-press.com

UI Elements

Image

Profil Image

Header/Title

Text

Primary Button

Secondary Button

Tertiary Button

BUTTON

BUTTON

BUTTON

Toggle

Check Boxes

Radio Buttons

Number Stepper

1

Search Bar

Text Input Field

Progress Bar

Slider

Volume Slider

Icons

Add	Add User	Attach	Alarm	Browser	Calendar

Camera	Cart	Close	Cloud	Cloud Share	Cloud Upload

Calculator	Comment	Compress	Copy	Credit-Card	Cursor

Cursor	Cut	Download	Document	Exclamation	Fingerprint

Heart	Hearts	Hide PW	Home	Hourglass	Incognito

Info	Left	Life-Ring	Link	List-Check	Lock

Mail	Map	Map-Marker	Mic	Music	New Mail

Pin	Power	Print	Question	Right	Search

Settings	Share	Shuffle	Signal	Sliders	Smile

Star	Support	Tag	Thumbtack	Thumbs-down	Thumbs-up

Trash	Unlock	Upload	User	Volume	Wink

Project
Title

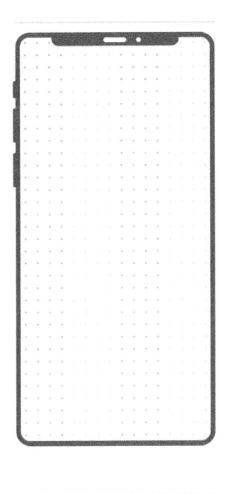
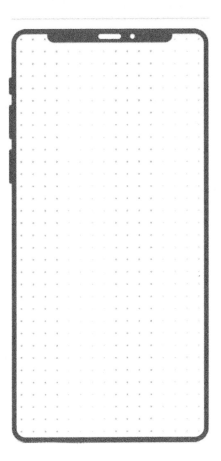
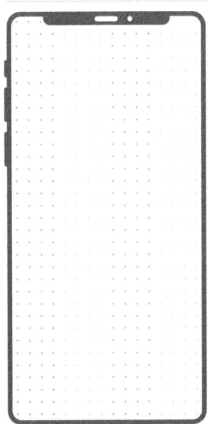
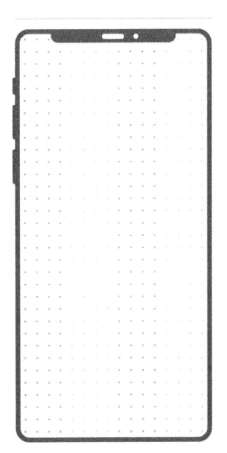

Project
Title

Project
Title

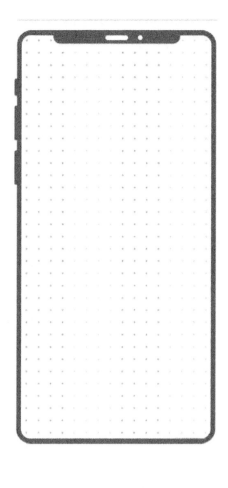

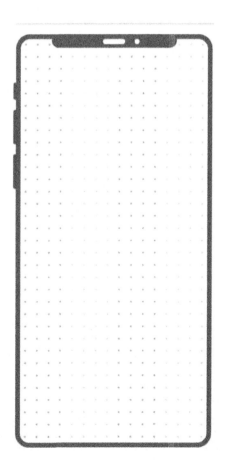

Project
Title

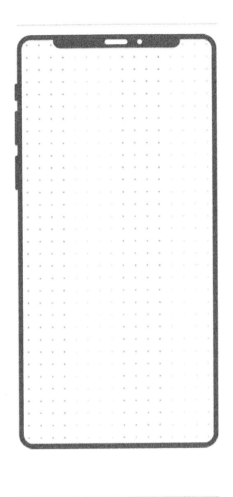

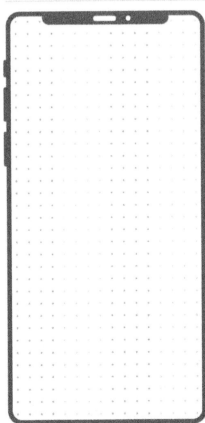
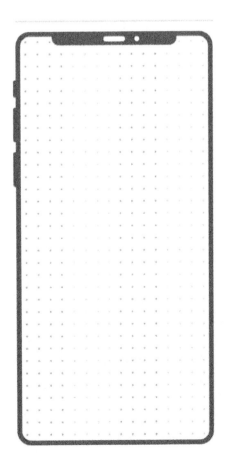

Project
Title

Project
Title

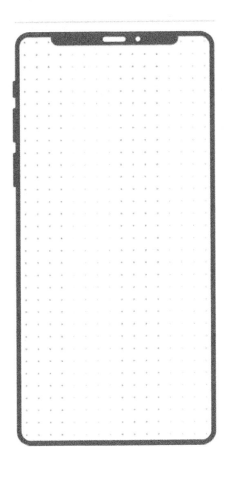
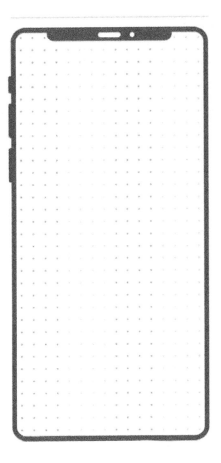

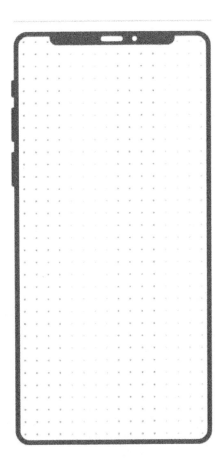

Project
Title

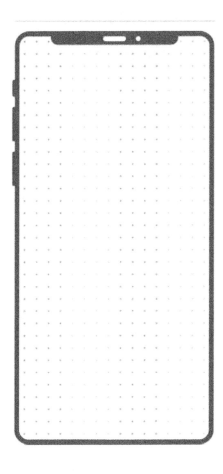
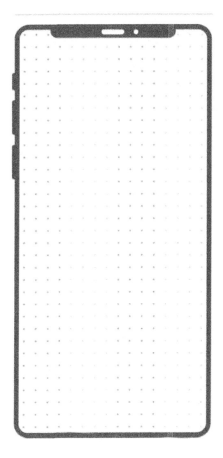
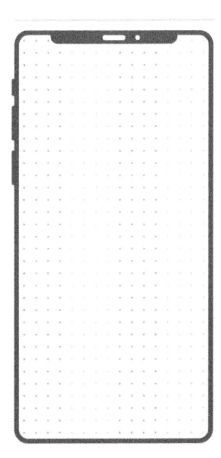
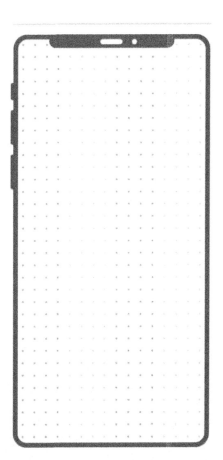

Project
Title

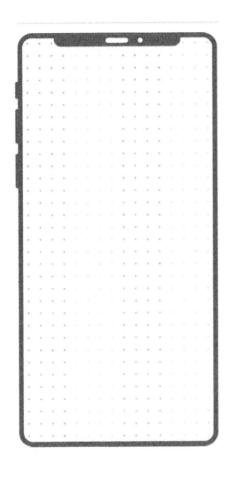
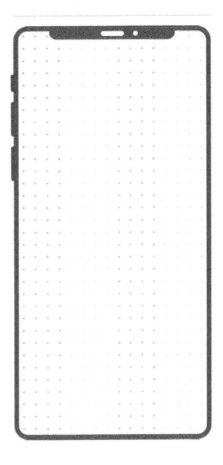

Project
Title

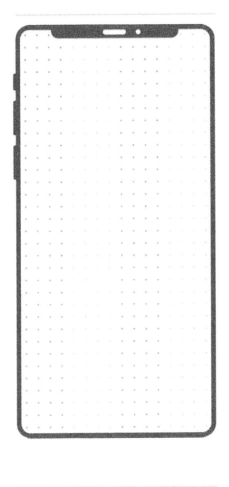
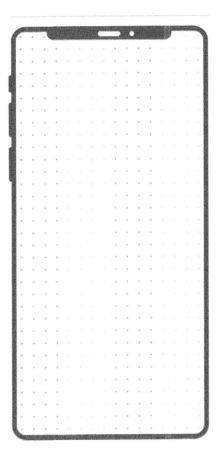

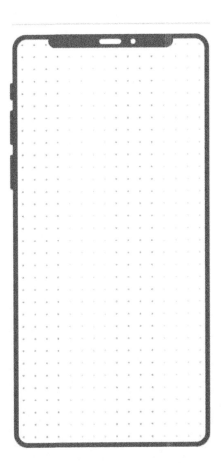

Project
Title

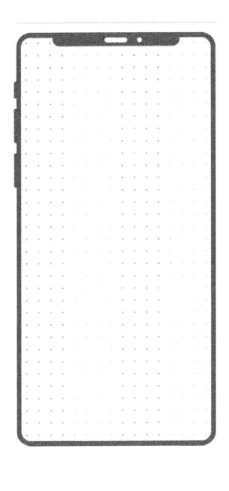
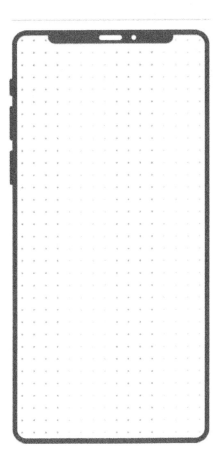
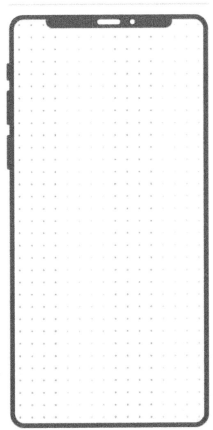
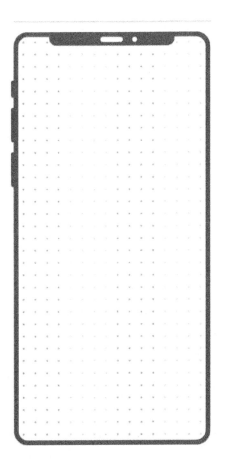

Project
Title

Project
Title

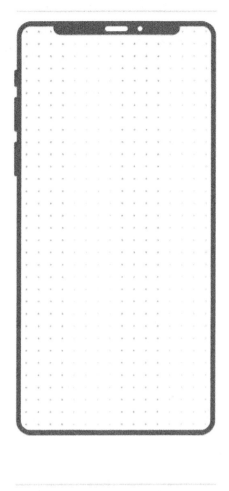
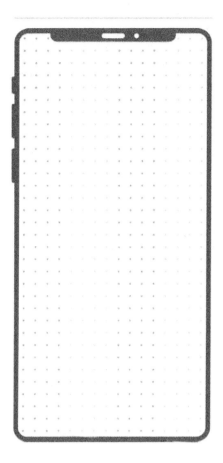

Project
Title

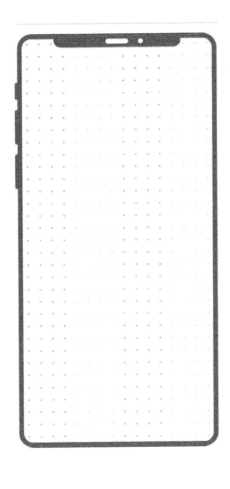
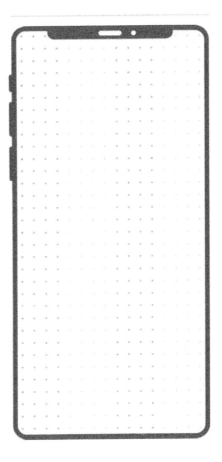

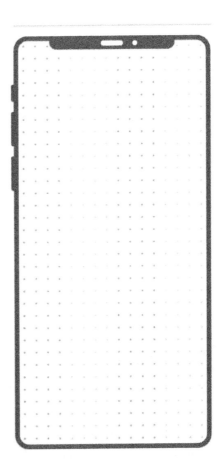

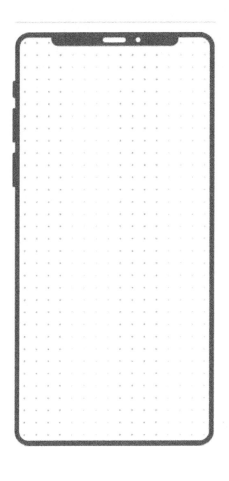
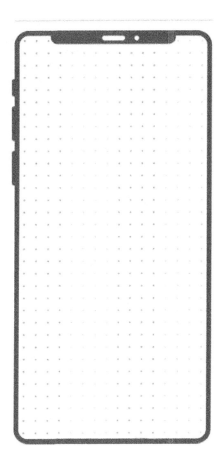
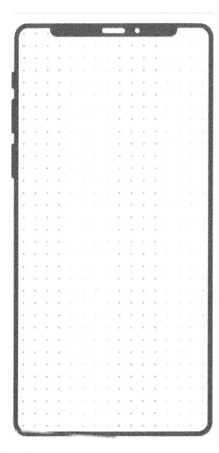
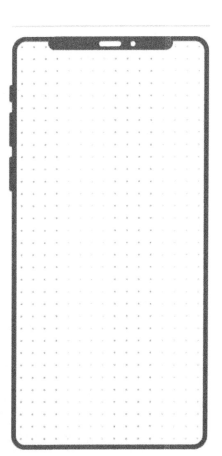

Project
Title

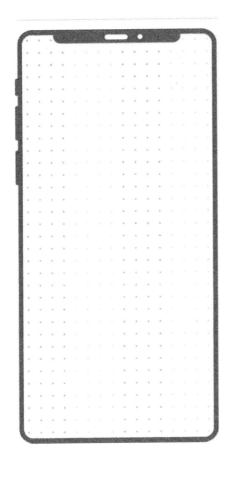

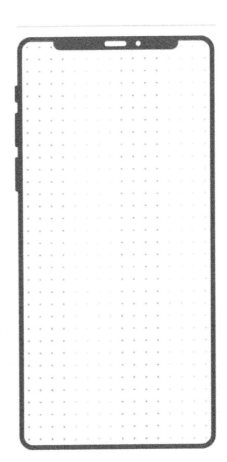

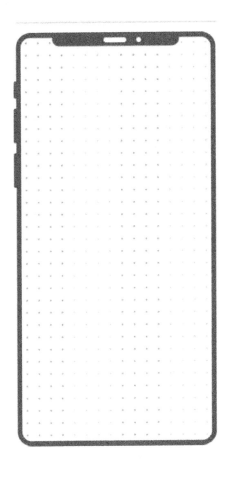

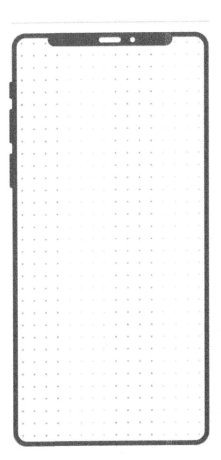

Project
Title

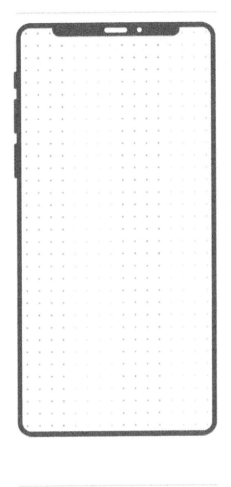
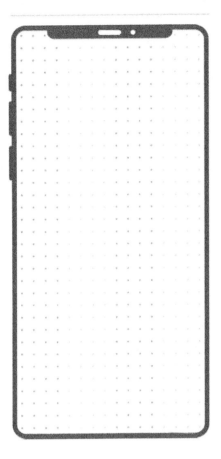

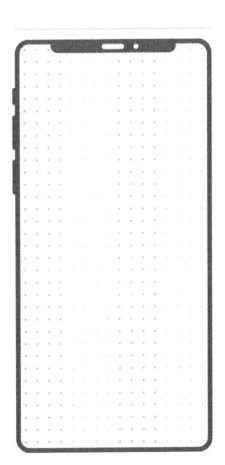

Project
Title

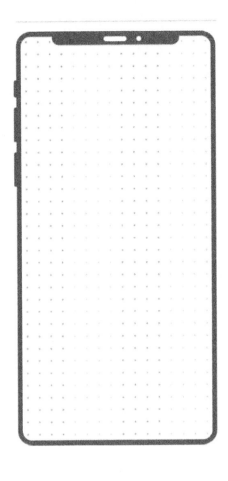

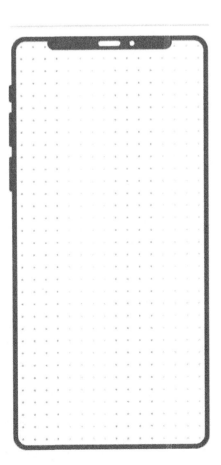

Project
Title

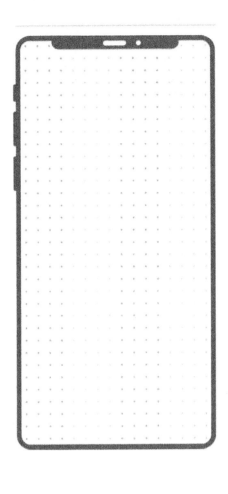

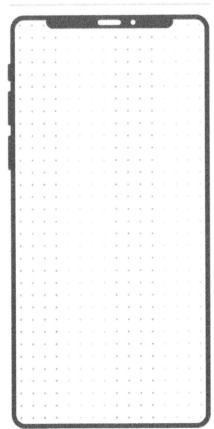
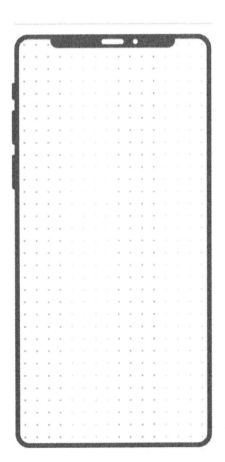

Project
Title

Project
Title

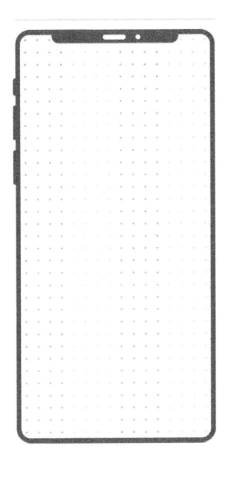
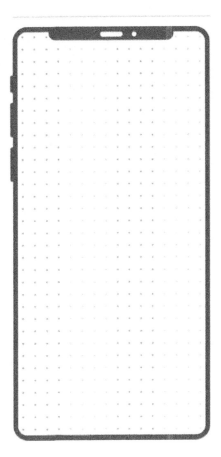

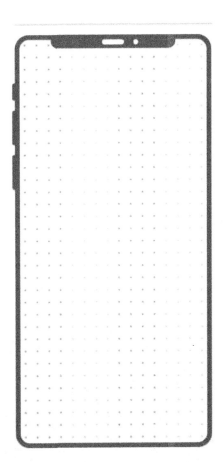

Project
Title

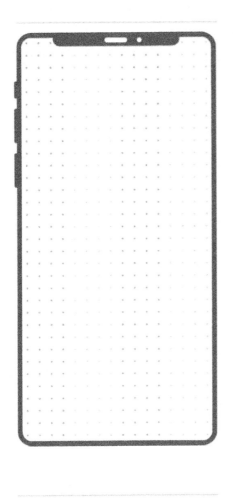
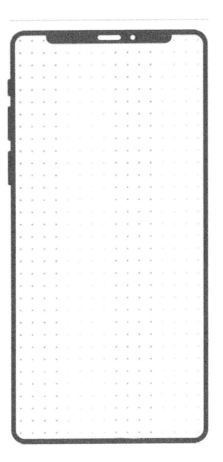
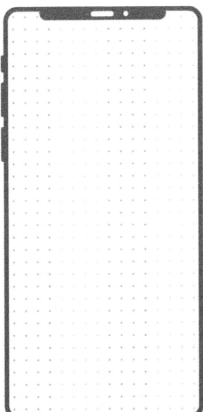

Project
Title

Project
Title

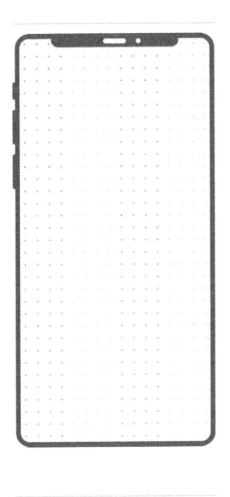
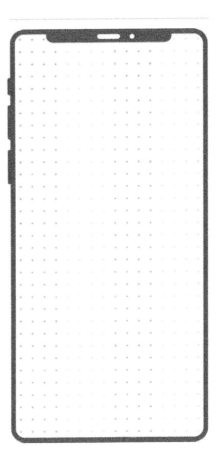

Project
Title

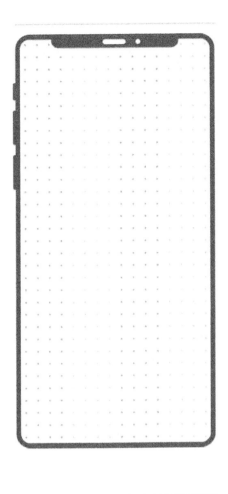
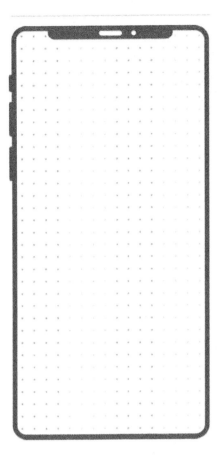
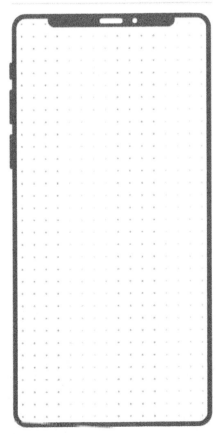
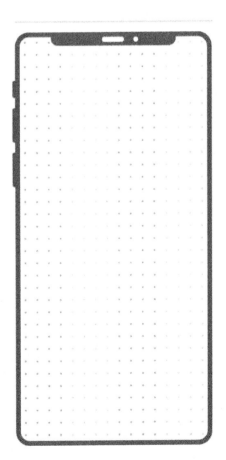

Project
Title

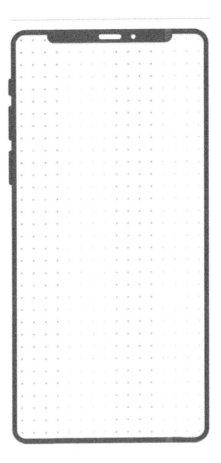

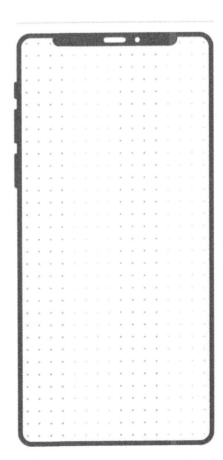

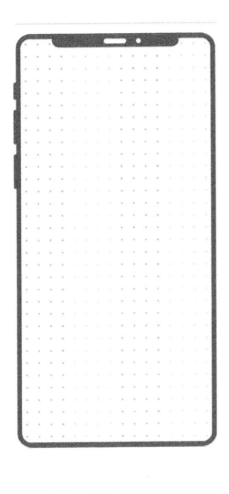
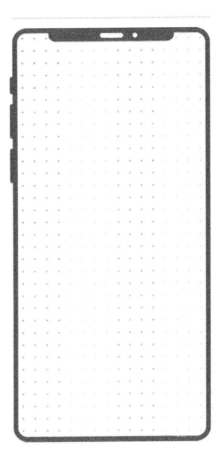
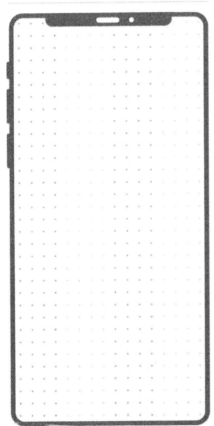
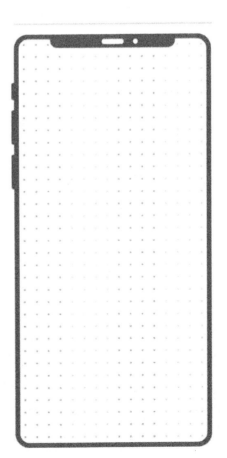

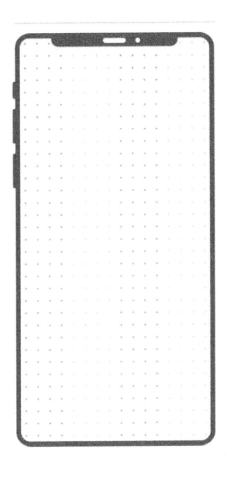
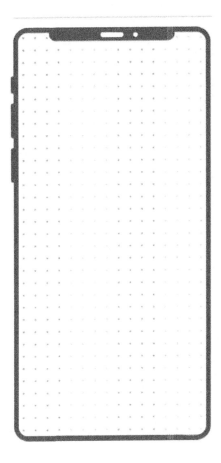
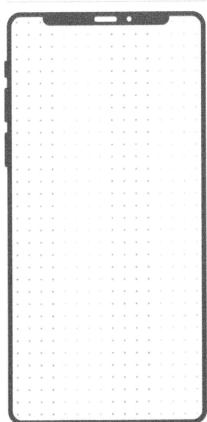
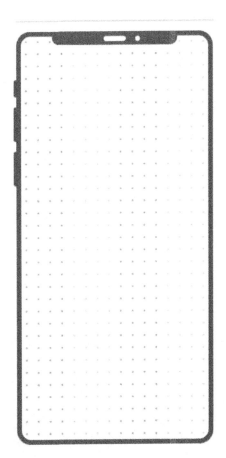

Project
Title

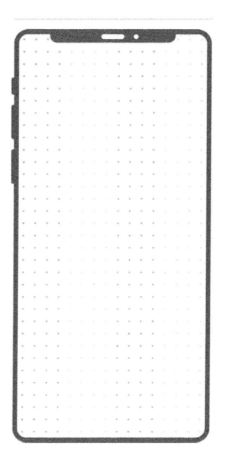

Project
Title

Project
Title

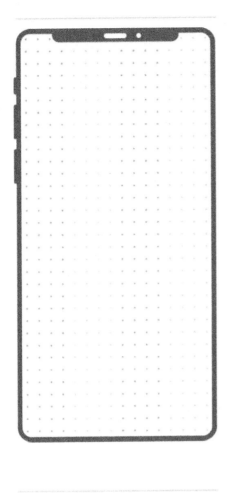
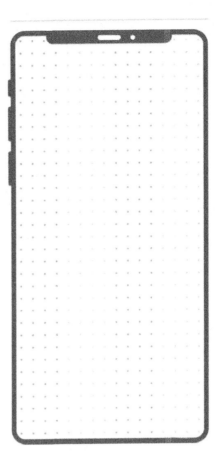

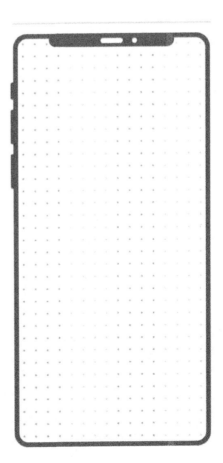

Project
Title

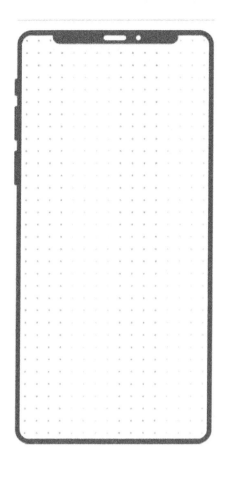

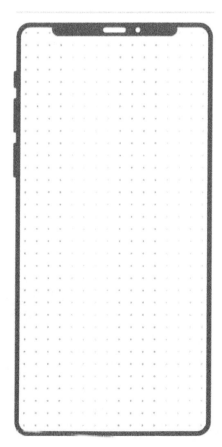
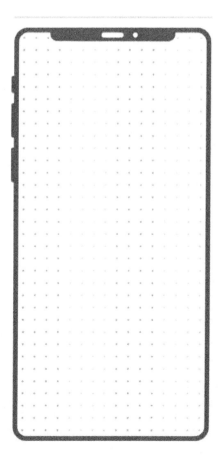

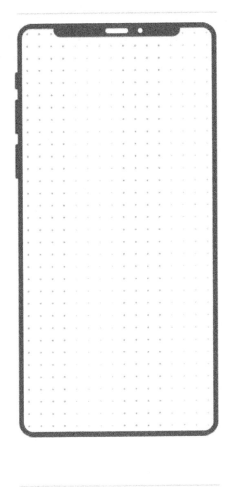

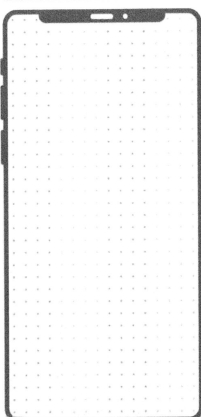
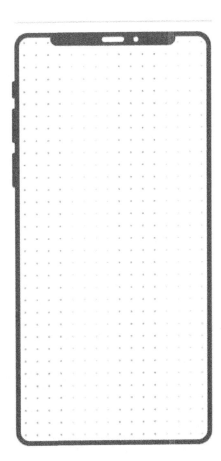

Project
Title

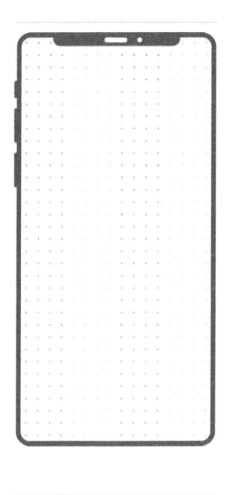
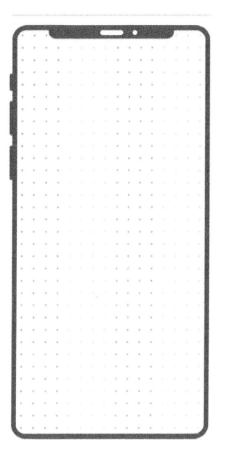
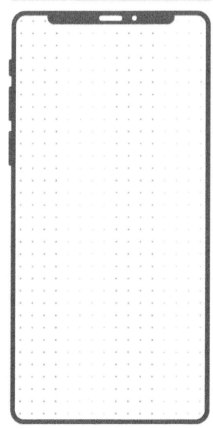
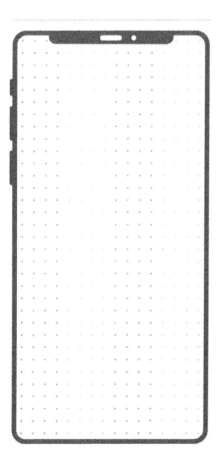

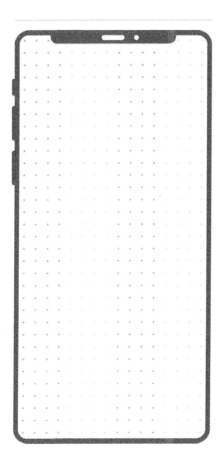
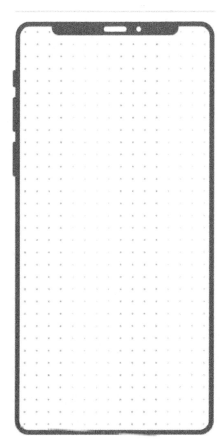
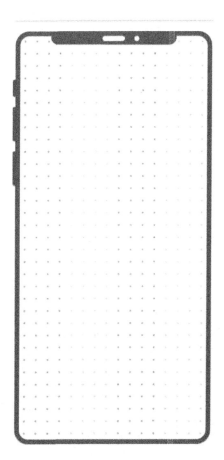

Project
Title

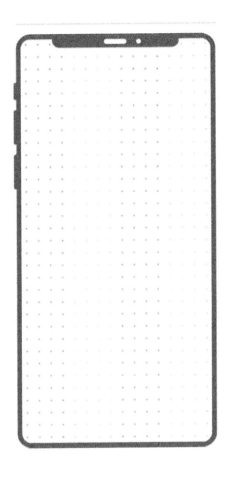
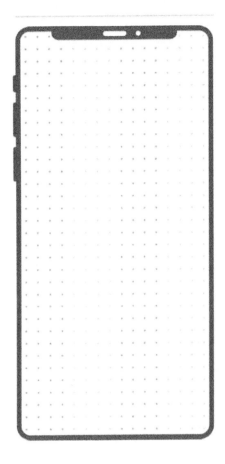

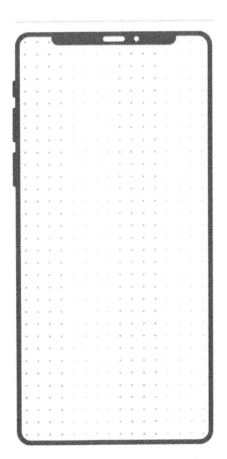

Project
Title

Project
Title

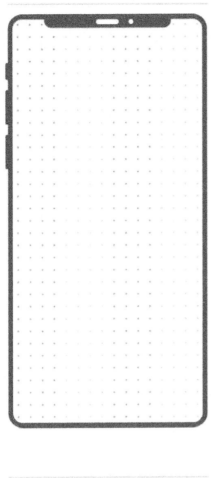
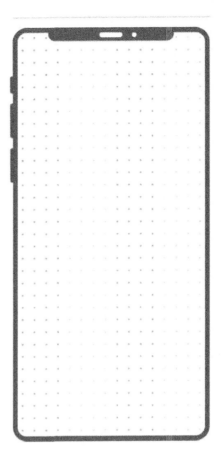

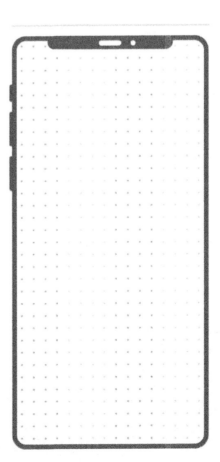

Project
Title

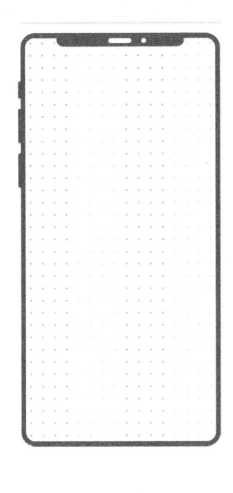
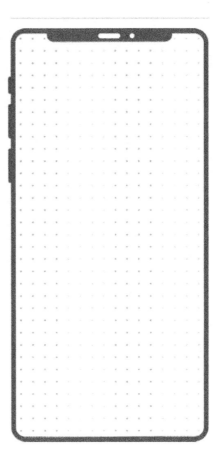
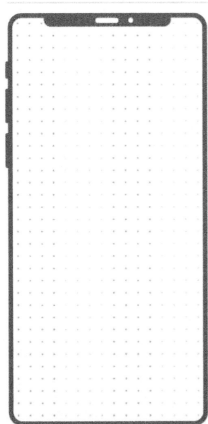
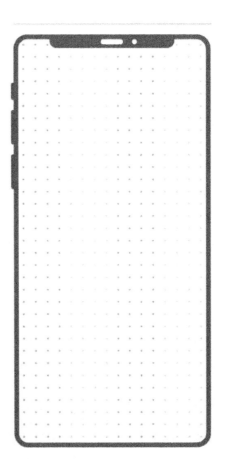

Project
Title

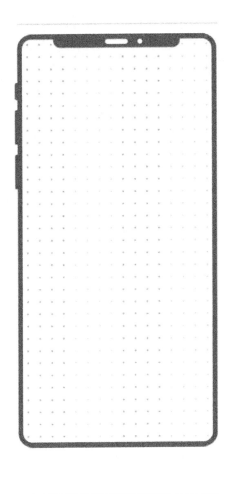
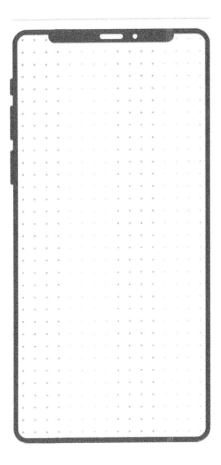
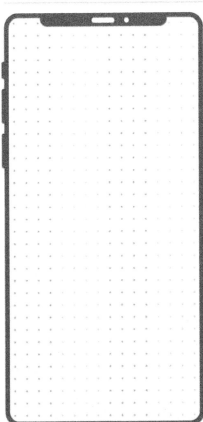

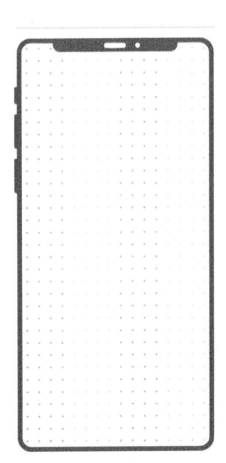

Project
Title

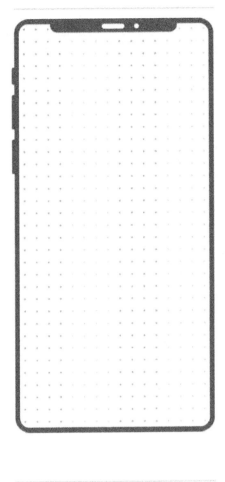

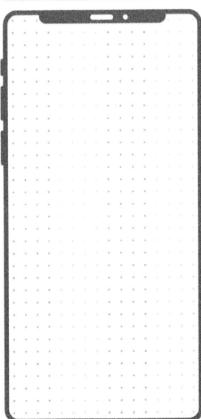

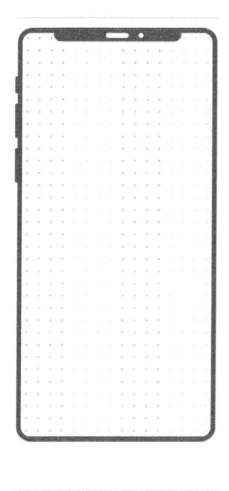

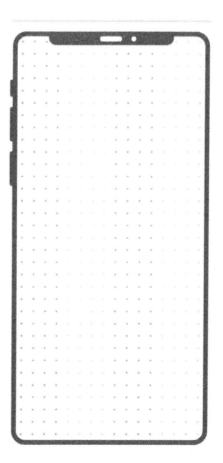

Project
Title

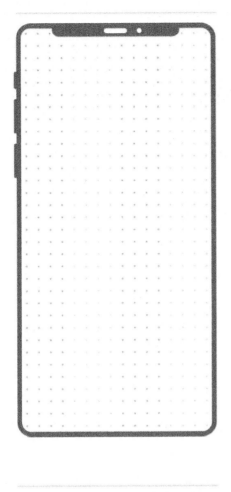
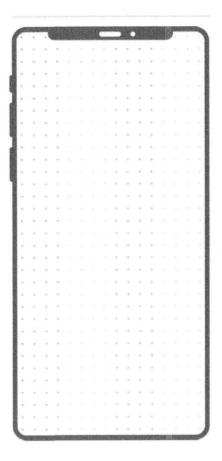

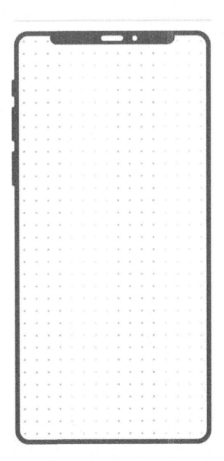

Project
Title

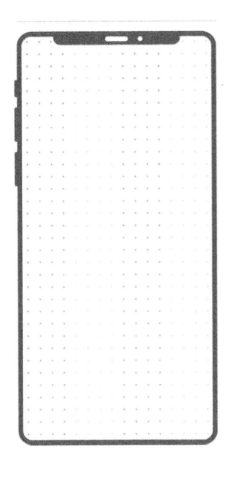

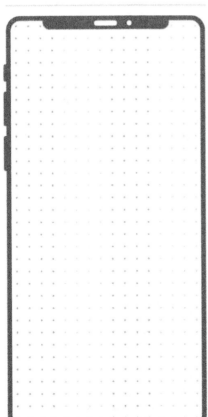

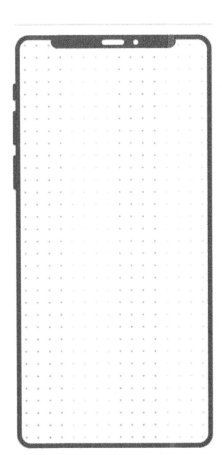

Project
Title

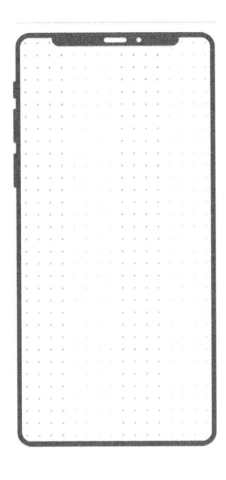

Project
Title

Project
Title

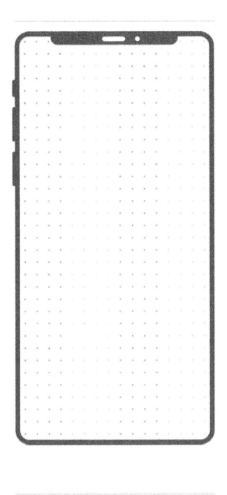
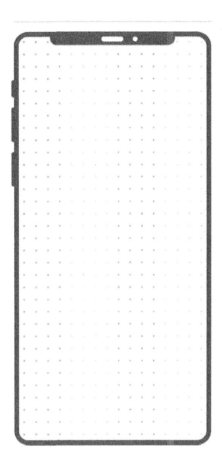

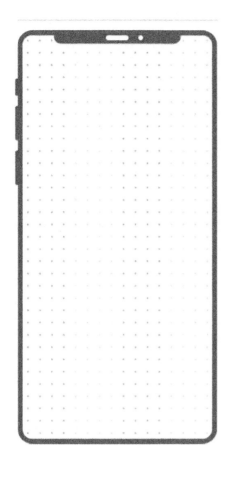
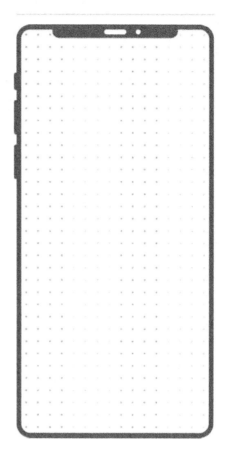
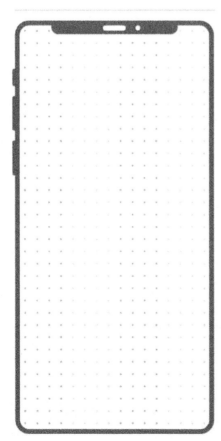

Project
Title

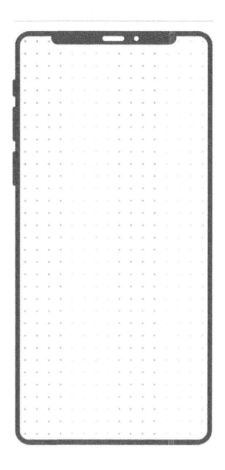

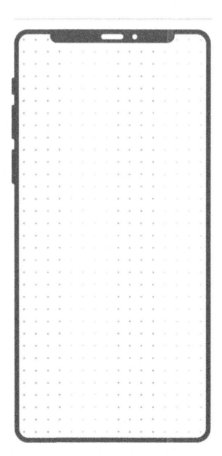

Project
Title

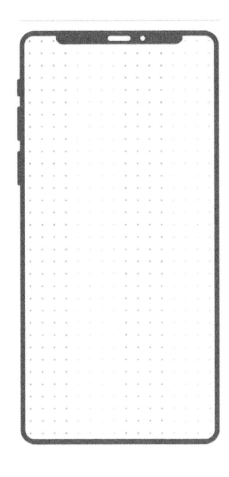
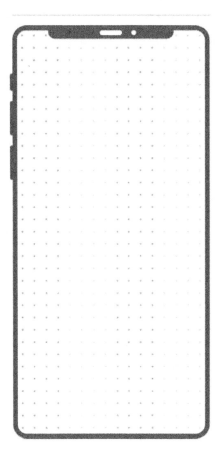
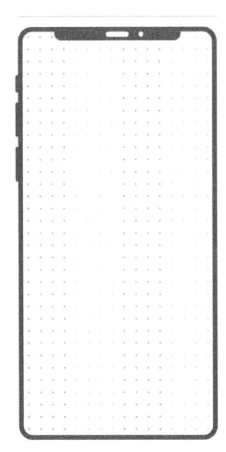
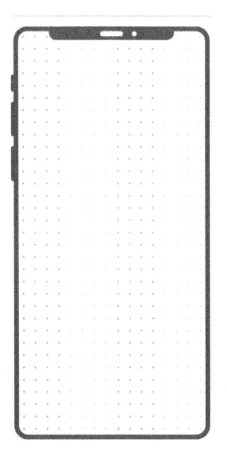

Project
Title

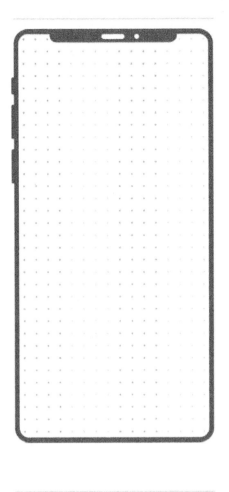

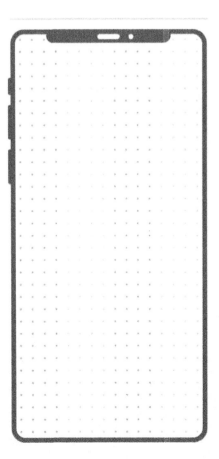

Project
Title

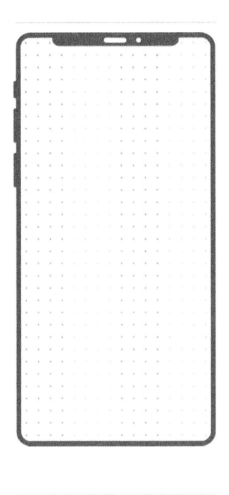
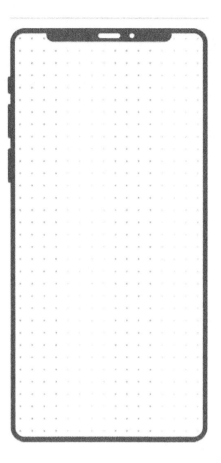

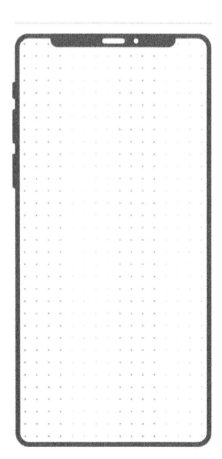

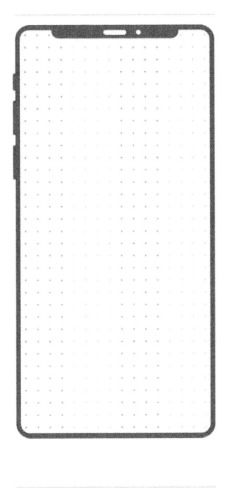
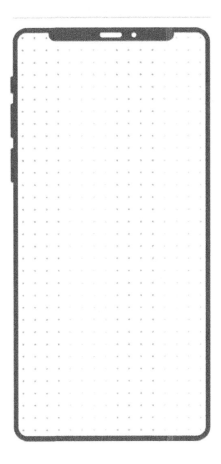

Project
Title

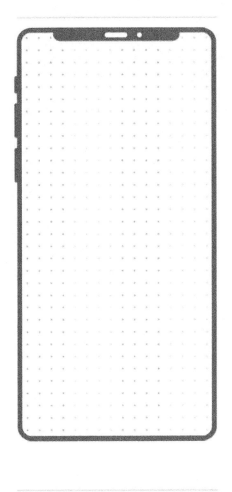

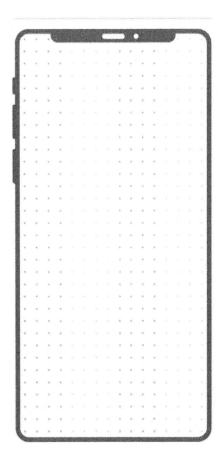

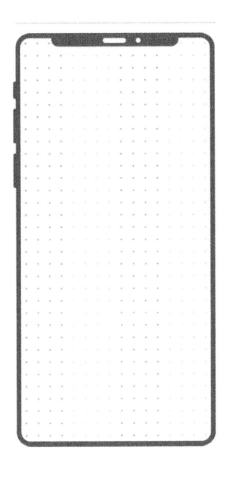
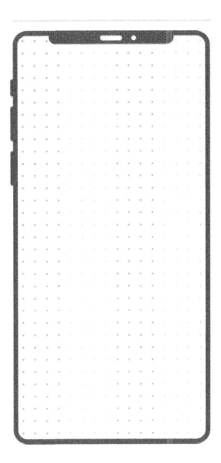
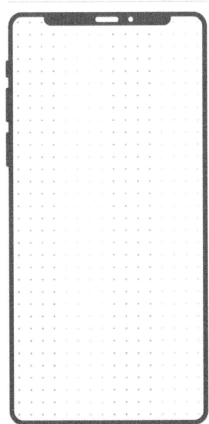
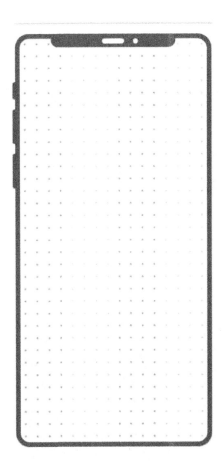

Project
Title

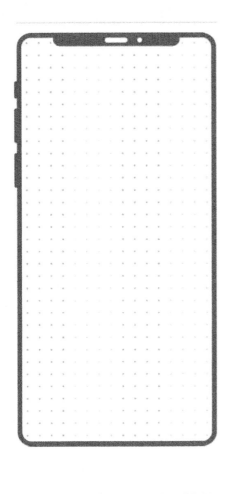
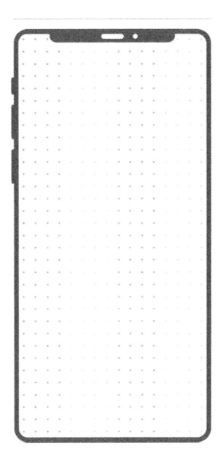

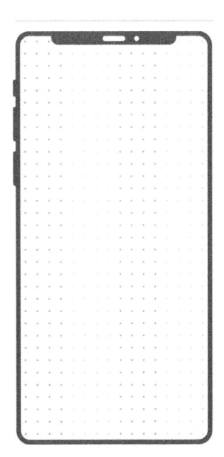

Project
Title

Project
Title

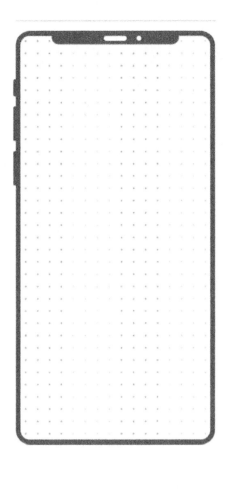

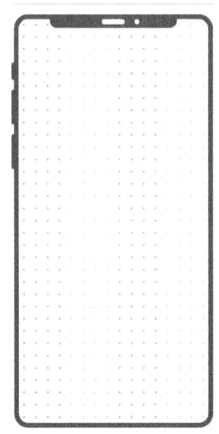
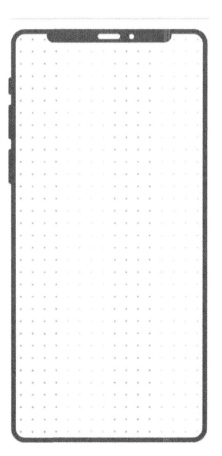

Project
Title

Project
Title

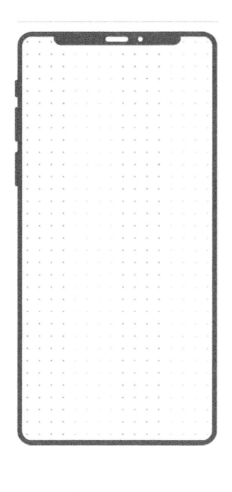
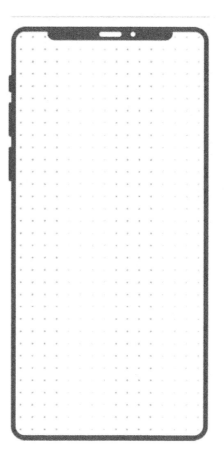

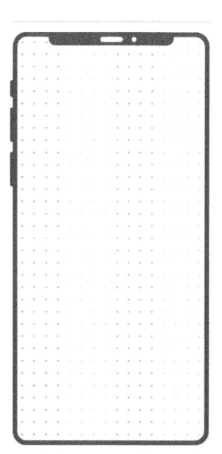

Project
Title

Project
Title

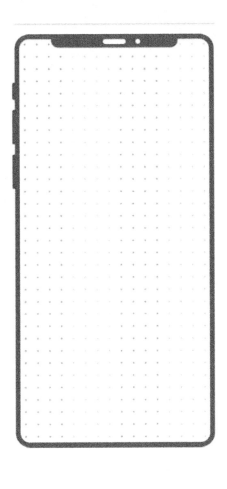
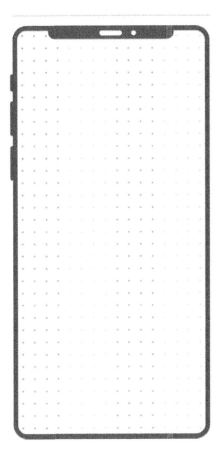
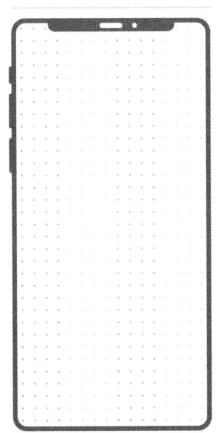

Made in United States
North Haven, CT
24 April 2022

18532598R00070